Welcome to Issue Five
The Promise Keeper

XTB stands for **eXplore The Bible**.

Read a bit of the Bible each day and...
- Zoom in on **Mark** to meet Jesus, the promised King.
- Journey to the Promised Land in **Numbers** and **Deuteronomy**.
- Read about God's promise and plan in Paul's letter to the **Ephesians**.

Are you ready to explore the Bible? Fill in the bookmark...
...then turn over the page to start exploring with XTB!

Table Talk FOR FAMILIES

Look out for **Table Talk** — a book to help children and adults explore the Bible together. It can be used by:

- Families
- One adult with one child
- Children's leaders with their groups
- Any other way you want to try

Table Talk uses the same Bible passages as XTB so that they can be used together if wanted. You can buy Table Talk from your local Good Book Company website:
UK: www.thegoodbook.co.uk • North America: www.thegoodbook.com
Australia: www.thegoodbook.com.au • New Zealand: www.thegoodbook.co.nz

C000271490

Sometimes I'm called

.... (nickname)

My birthday is

....

My age is

....

I look

like this:

How to find your way around the Bible.

Look out for the READ sign.
It tells you what Bible bit to read.

READ
Mark 1v2-6

So, if the notes say... READ Mark 1v2-6
...this means chapter 1 and verses 2 to 6
...and this is how you find it.

Use the **Contents** page in your Bible to
find where Mark begins

The chapter numbers
are the **GREAT BIG**
ones

The verse numbers are the
tiny ones!

Oops! Keep getting lost?
Cut out this bookmark and use it to keep your place.

How to use xtb

1 Find a time and place when you can read the Bible each day.

2 Get your Bible, a pencil and your XTB notes.

3 Ask God to help you to understand what you read.

4 Read today's XTB page and Bible bit.

5 Pray about what you have read and learned.

6 If you can, talk to an adult or a friend about what you've learned.

YOUR FREE XTB PRAYER DIARY

This copy of XTB comes with a free **Prayer Diary**.

When we talk to God He <u>always</u> listens! Your prayer diary has loads of ideas for different ways of talking to God. You can use it keep a record of His answers too.

As we explore Mark, Numbers, Deuteronomy and Ephesians, there'll be plenty to talk to God about.

Are you ready to start? Then hurry on to Day 1.

DAY 1 MARK TIME

Welcome to Mark's book about Jesus.
It's divided into two halves:

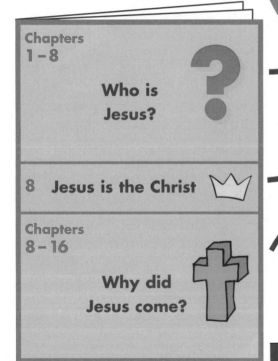

Chapters 1–8

Who is Jesus?

8 Jesus is the Christ

Chapters 8–16

Why did Jesus come?

Mark starts his book by telling us <u>who</u> Jesus is.
He is **"Jesus Christ, the Son of God."** (Mark 1v1)
Mark then spends the first half of the book (chapters 1–8) giving us *evidence* that Jesus really <u>is</u> the Christ, the Son of God.

Christ means "God's Chosen King".
The Old Testament is full of promises about a new King.
Mark shows us that **Jesus** is this promised King.

What kind of King is Jesus?
The people wanted a warrior king, who would fight the Romans. But Jesus was a very different kind of King.
He is the King who came to **die!**
Mark explains <u>why</u> Jesus came—and why He had to die—in the second half of his book.

Did you know?

When Mark wrote his book, he wrote it in a language called Greek. It looks like this: αλισον μιτχηελλ. Mark's book didn't have chapters and verses—or headings. These were added later to make it easier for us to find our way around the book.

DAY 1
CONTINUED

GOOD NEWS!

Verse 1 of Mark's book is like a heading. It tells us what his book is about.

Take the first letter of each picture to discover Mark's heading for his book.

The beginning of the G O S P E L

of J E S U S   C H R I S T,

the S O N of g o d .

Gospel means "Good News". The news Mark is giving us isn't bad—or boring! It's <u>good</u> news!

READ
Mark 1v1

Mark is introducing us to **Jesus**. It's as if Mark is talking to us like this:

> I want you to meet my friend, Jesus.

> Actually, He's the King. And He's God!

What amazing claims!
As we read Mark together we'll look at his evidence, and see <u>why</u> he believes these incredible things about Jesus.

PRAY **Ask God to help you to learn more about who Jesus is and why He came as you read Mark's book.**

DAY 2 ROYAL MESSENGER

Mark 1v2-5

Crack the code to see three promises from the Old Testament.

⇨=C ⇩=E ⇦=G ⬆=I ➡=K
⬇=M ⬁=N ◁=R ▷=S ▽=U

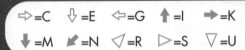

K I N G

God promised to send a new King.

R E S C U E R

This King would rescue His people.

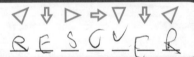

M E S S E N G E R

God promised to send a messenger first, to tell the people **"Get ready for the King"**.

READ
Mark 1v2-5

Which promise does God keep in these verses?

His promise to send the
King/Rescuer/Messenger

Who did God send as the promised messenger? (v4)

J ~~ohn~~ the Baptist

John knew the people <u>weren't ready</u> for their King. They hadn't been living the way God wanted them to.

What did John tell them to do? (v4)
Cross out the X's

T~~x~~ur~~xx~~n a~~xx~~wa~~x~~y ~~x~~fr~~x~~om~~x~~ ~~xx~~si~~x~~n,
a~~x~~n~~xx~~d ~~x~~b~~x~~e b~~x~~ap~~x~~tis~~xx~~ed~~x~~.

John baptised people in the river Jordan. It showed that they wanted to be washed clean from all their wrongs (their sins), ready to welcome King Jesus.

PRAYER DIARY

God sent John as His messenger—just as He had promised. Thank God that He <u>always</u> keeps His promises. (*That's why this issue of XTB is called "The Promise-Keeper". Find out more on **page 3** of your XTB Prayer Diary.*)

THE KING IS COMING

Yesterday we met the **royal messenger**.
Now it's time to hear his message.

READ
Mark 1v6-8

Circle ten mistakes in the story.

(Mark) wore clothes made of (hamster) (hair), with a (plastic) belt round his waist. His food was (scorpions) and (tame) honey. He told the people, "The man who will come (before) me is much (less) important than I am. I am not good enough even to bend down and (untie his trainers). I baptise you with (lemonade), but he will baptise you with (water)."

Copy out what verse 8 really says:

I baptise you with water, but he

baptise you with the holy spirit!

When John baptised people, he just washed them on the <u>outside</u>. But Jesus would give His **Spirit** to His followers, to live <u>in them</u> and help them to live for Jesus.

Did you know?

The Old Testament promises about the royal messenger say that he will be like **Elijah**, an Old Testament prophet. (A prophet is God's messenger). Elijah wore hair clothing, with a leather belt. (2 Kings 1v8) So did John the Baptist!

What has John told us about Jesus?

Use these words to fill in the gaps.

Spirit   greater

    sandals   Holy

- Jesus is much *greater* than John.
- John's not worthy to untie Jesus' *sandals*
- Jesus will baptise with the ~~Holy~~ *Holy Spirit*

At another time, John also said this about Jesus:

"He must become greater; I must become less." John 3v30

PRAY

Do you see how great Jesus is? Praise Him now. Ask Him to help you to see His greatness more as you read Mark's book.

THE KING IS BAPTISED

John had been baptising people in the river Jordan. Then **Jesus** came to be baptised as well.

Spot six differences between the two baptisms.

This is my Son.

READ
Mark 1v9-

There's <u>another</u> difference, that you can't see in the pictures.

The people who came to John to be baptised admitted that they were sinful and needed to be forgiven. John baptised **sinners** who **repented** (turned away from their sins).

But **Jesus** was very different. He lived a **perfect** life. He <u>never</u> sinned, and had no need to repent. Jesus was baptised to **please** God. It was all part of God's plan.

As Jesus came up out of the water, God spoke from heaven. What did He say? (v11)

pleased
Son
love

You are my _Son_, whom I _love_, with you I am well _pleased_.

Jesus is God's Son. God loves Jesus and delights in Him.

But, as we saw on Day 1, Jesus is the King who came to <u>die</u>! God sent His greatly loved Son to rescue us by dying in our place, so that our sins can be forgiven. That's how much God loves us!

We'll find out more about how Jesus rescues us from sin on Day 12.

PRAY Thank God for sending His perfect, loved Son to be your Rescuer.

DAY 5 TEMPTING TIMES

Mark is giving us <u>evidence</u> that Jesus is the Christ, the Son of God (v1). *Solve the puzzle to see the evidence so far.*

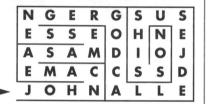

N	G	E	R	G	S	U	S
E	S	S	E	O	H	N	E
A	S	A	M	D	I	O	J
E	M	A	C	C	S	S	D
J	O	H	N	A	L	L	E

Start here →

Copy the letters as you go through the maze.

JOHN CAME AS A MESSENGER. GOD CALLED JESUS HIS SON

READ
Mark 1v12-13

Who sent Jesus into the desert? (v12)

The holy spirit

How long was Jesus there? (v13)

40 Days + 40 nights

Who was with Jesus? (v13)

- S aten _____ (the devil)
- W ild animal _____
- A ngels _____

Did you know?

Satan always wants to <u>spoil</u> God's good plans. God had sent Jesus as His chosen King (the Christ), to rescue His people. Satan would try anything to stop Jesus.

But Jesus is **perfect**! He <u>didn't</u> give in to Satan, the tempter.

You can read this story in more detail in Matthew 4v1-11.

Later on in Mark we'll see that Satan tries other ways to stop Jesus. But he can't. God's plans <u>can't</u> be stopped!

THINK + PRAY

The devil is sometimes called the <u>tempter</u>. He tempts us to do things which displease God—and is delighted when we give in. The Bible promises that God will always help us when tempted. He will give us a way out. *This promise is in 1 Corinthians 10v13.* Talk to God about this. Ask Him to help <u>you</u> when tempted.

DAY 6 — THE TIME HAS COME

xtb — Mark 1v14-15

Quick Quiz
Answers at bottom of page.

1 Where was Jesus born? **B**ethlehem

2 Where did He grow up? **N**azareth

3 Where was He baptised by John?
The river **J**ordan

4 Where did He go to be tempted?
Into the **d**esert

Find all these places on the map.

MAP OF ISRAEL
IN NEW TESTAMENT TIMES

(Map labels: Mediteranean Sea, Capernaum, Sea of Galilee, GALILEE, Nazareth, SAMARIA, DECAPOLIS, River Jordan, Jerusalem, PEREA, JUDEA, Bethlehem, Dead Sea, DESERT)

READ
Mark 1v14-15

What happened to John the Baptist? (v14)

He was put in **p**rison

Where did Jesus go? (v14) **G**alilee

*Draw a (circle) round **Galilee** on the map.*

What was Jesus' message? (v15)

The **t**ime has come.

The **k**ingdom of God is **n**ear.
Repent and **b**elieve the good news!

Did you know?

The Kingdom of God isn't a ***place***—like Wales or Australia! It's ***people***, who have Jesus as their King, ruling over them.

The Kingdom of God is <u>near</u> because Jesus the King has arrived. People must **repent** (turn away from sin) and **believe** the good news about Jesus.

We'll find out more about this on Day 12.

PRAY — Thank God for keeping His promise to send Jesus as King.

Answers: 1 Bethlehem, 2 Nazareth, 3 River Jordan, 4 The desert.

DAY 7 FOLLOW ME

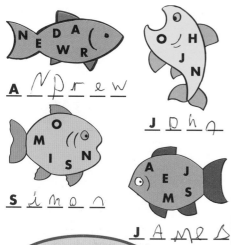

Follow me, and I will make you fishers of men.

Who was Jesus talking to? *Unjumble the letters on each fish to find four names.*

A _N_d_r_e_w_

J _D_h_n_

S _i_m_o_n_

J _A_M_E_S_

READ
Mark 1v16-20

Jesus was by the **Sea of Galilee** (sometimes called Lake Galilee). *Find it on yesterday's map.*

The men Jesus spoke to were **fishermen**. But what did Jesus say they would do instead? (v17)

FISH__MEN!

This didn't mean catching people in a large net! It means telling people about Jesus the King, so that they can start to follow Him too.

How quickly did these men go with Jesus? (v18 & 20)

At once / In a few days / Weeks later

xtb Mark 1v16-20

Spot the Evidence

In the next few days, we'll see Jesus' amazing **authority**. (*That means He is in charge.*) Mark will show us that Jesus has the same authority as God—evidence that Jesus **is** the Son of God.

- **Today's** story shows that Jesus has authority over **people**—these fishermen left their jobs straight away.

- **Tomorrow** we'll see what else Jesus is in charge of.

THINK + PRAY

These fishermen became Jesus' followers. They followed Jesus all their lives—and told others about Him too. Are you a follower of Jesus? Do you want to tell your friends about Him? Talk to God about your answers. Ask Him to help you.

DAY 8 · WHO'S IN CHARGE?

Mark is still giving us **evidence** that Jesus has the same **authority** as God. (He's <u>in charge</u>.)

Jesus went to the Jewish meeting place (the synagogue) on the <u>Sabbath</u> (*the Jewish day of rest*).

> *Look out for "authority" as you read the verses.*

READ
Mark 1v21-28

What kind of *authority* did Jesus have?

Verse 22
Authority as a t *eacher*

Verse 26
Authority over e *very* s *pirit*

> **Did you know?**
> Sometimes in the Bible we read about evil spirits. They are God's enemies, and often made people ill. But **God** is <u>far</u> more powerful than any evil spirit!

When Jesus commanded the evil spirit to leave the man, what happened? (v26)

 I left, BYE!

 Wow!

Jesus was **in charge**. The evil spirit <u>had</u> to obey Him!

Read verse 27 again.

How did the people feel about Jesus?

AMAZED

THINK SPOT

Are you **amazed** by Jesus? Why / why not?

PRAY

As we read Mark's book, we'll be reading Jesus' amazing teaching for ourselves. Do <u>you</u> want to listen to Jesus—and do what He says? Talk to Him about it now.

DAY 9 NAY FEVER!

Simon and Andrew lived in **Capernaum**, a fishing village on the shore of the Sea of Galilee. *Find it on the map on Day 6.*

READ
Mark 1v29-34

Jesus and His disciples went to the home of **Simon** and Andrew in **Capernaum**. Simon's **mother-in-law** was sick in bed with a **fever**. Jesus went to her, took her by the hand and helpéd her up. **Straight** away the fever left her. Later that evening, the whole **town** came to the house. They brought all the **sick** people, and those who had evil spirits in them. Jesus **healed** many people, and made the evil spirits leave.

Find all the red words in the wordsearch. Some are written backwards!

S	T	R	A	I	G	H	T	N	W	O	T
S	M	O	T	H	E	R	I	N	L	A	W
I	C	F	E	V	E	R	N	O	M	I	S
K	C	I	S	K	N	H	E	A	L	E	D
C	A	P	E	R	N	A	U	M	E	S	S

 xtb

Mark
1v29-34

 Spot the Evidence

This time, Jesus shows another kind of **authority**. Copy the leftover letters (in order) from the wordsearch to see what else Jesus has authority over.

  S I C K N E S S

Only **God** has complete control over sickness. But Jesus has the <u>same</u> authority—because He is the **Son of God**.

 Wow! There were many other sick people in Israel. Jesus <u>didn't</u> heal all of them—but He <u>could</u> have done! He is in charge over sickness.

 PRAYER DIARY

Do you know someone who is ill? Who? _Nanny_

Pray for them now. **Page 4** of your **XTB Prayer Diary** will help you.

PRAYING AND PREACHING

What time did you get up today? *Draw the time on the clock face.*

Jesus had an exhausting evening, healing loads of people. A lie-in in the morning might have been nice. But instead He got up really early...

READ
Mark 1v35-39

It was still dark—long before sunrise. There must have been a really good reason for getting up so early!

Find it at the end of verse 35.

To p⊿⋀⋁

Jesus wanted to speak to God, His Father. That was more important than sleeping in!

THINK SPOT

- When do <u>you</u> pray?
- Do you just squeeze in a quick prayer if there's time?
- Would you get up early to speak to God— even if you were tired?

Simon and the others had to search for Jesus.

Everyone's looking for you!

THINK SPOT

Think back to yesterday's story. Why do you think everyone's looking for Jesus?

But Jesus wouldn't stay in Capernaum. He had to visit the other towns in Galilee as well. Why? (v38)

To p_reach_

If you have time, check back to verse 15 to see what Jesus was preaching.

PRAYER DIARY

Look back to the **Think Spot**. Prayer <u>mattered</u> to Jesus. It matters for you too! When's a good time for <u>you</u> to pray? (*The front of your Prayer Diary has some ideas on how to pray.*) Ask God to help you to spend time talking to Him **every day**.

Have you ever been ill with something catching, like Chicken Pox?

It's horrid isn't it? You feel rotten. You're bored. And your friends can't come round in case they catch it too.

Did You Know?

In Bible times, people sometimes caught a horrible skin disease called **leprosy**. Nobody wanted to be mates with a leper—in case they caught it too. You had to leave your home and friends. You could <u>never</u> come back—unless the priest checked you and said you were no longer ill.

READ
Mark 1v40-45

Crack the code to see what Jesus did.

☆=A ☆=C ✪=D ☆=E ★=H
☆=L ✳=O ☆=R ✱=T ✪=U

☆ ✳ ☆ ☆ ✪

Jesus _c a r e d_ about him. (v41)

No one else did.

✱ ✳ ✪ ☆ ★ ☆ ✪

Jesus _Touched_ him. (v41)

No one else would.

★ ☆ ☆ ★ ☆ ✪

Jesus _Healed_ him. (v42)

No one else could!

Jesus touched this man (probably the first time in ages that anyone had touched him). And Jesus cured him!

But there was a price to pay...

What did the man do? (v45)

Told no one/Told a few/Told everyone

Crowds flocked to Jesus to see more miracles. But that <u>wasn't</u> why Jesus came. He came to **preach** (as we saw yesterday, v38)—but now He had to stay away from the towns because of the crowds.

PRAY

In some countries, leprosy is still a big problem today—especially in India, Brazil and Indonesia. Pray for **The Leprosy Mission**, a Christian charity, and for the people they help. *You can find out more at www.leprosymission.org*

DOWN HE CAME...

Imagine the scene.
You're squashed into a room, listening to Jesus. The place is packed. No room for anyone else. Jesus is a <u>great</u> teacher, so you're listening hard, when suddenly...

...a bit of ceiling lands on your head!

You look up, and see a small hole. Then a hand pops through, and rips a bit of the roof off! Yank! Tug! Pull! Now there's a H-U-G-E hole—and something's coming through it...

READ
Mark 2v1-5

This man was paralysed. He couldn't walk. What do you think his friends wanted Jesus to do?

heal him

What did Jesus say to him? (v5)

Son, your sins are forgiven

That's odd! If the man needed to <u>walk</u>, why did Jesus talk to him about <u>sin</u>?!

Did you know?

Sin is more than just doing wrong things. Sin is doing what **we** want instead of what **God** wants. Sin separates us from God.

THINK SPOT

This man couldn't walk—but he had a far bigger problem. His BIGGEST problem was *sin*.

The great news is that Jesus came to <u>solve</u> the problem of sin.
*Read **The Servant King** on the next page to find out more.*

Time to Think
• Have **you** been forgiven by Jesus?
• Do you want to be?
(*If you're not sure, read **The Servant King** again.*)

PRAY

Father God, thank you that you love me so much that you sent Jesus to rescue me. Amen

THE SERVANT KING

How does Jesus solve the problem of sin? It's explained later in Mark's book. Jesus says that He...

> **...did not come to be served, but to serve, and to give his life as a ransom for many. (*Mark 10v45*)**

Jesus is the **Christ**—God's Chosen King. And He's the **Son of God**. He's awesome! He's in charge of everything. **BUT** He came as a <u>servant</u>! To help and save us. He loves us so much that He came to <u>rescue</u> us from our sin.

Why do we need rescuing?
Sin gets in the way between us and God. It stops us from knowing Him and stops us being His friends. The final result of sin is death. You can see why we need rescuing!

How did Jesus rescue us?
At the first Easter, when Jesus was about 33 years old, He was crucified. He was nailed to a cross and left to die.

As He died, all the sins of the world (all the wrongs people do) were put onto Jesus. He took all of our sin onto Himself, taking the punishment we deserve.

A ***ransom*** is money paid to set people free. Jesus died in our place, as our ransom—buying our freedom. <u>Jesus</u> paid the price for <u>our</u> sins.

When Jesus died, He dealt with the problem of sin. That means there is <u>nothing</u> to separate us from God any more. That's great news for you and me!

> We can know God today as our Friend and King— and one day live in heaven with Him for ever.

Did you know?

Jesus died on the cross as our Rescuer—but He didn't stay dead! After three days, God brought Him back to life! Jesus is still alive today, ruling as our King.

Have YOU been rescued by Jesus? Turn to the next page to find out more...

AM I A CHRISTIAN?

Not sure if you're a Christian? Then check it out below...

> **Christians are people who have been rescued by Jesus and follow Him as King.**

> **You can't become a Christian by trying to be good.**

That's great news, since you can't be totally good all the time!

It's about accepting what Jesus did on the cross to rescue you. To do that, you will need to **ABCD**.

A **Admit** your sin—that you do, say and think wrong things. Tell God you are sorry. Ask Him to forgive you, and to help you to change. There will be some wrong things you have to stop doing.

B **Believe** that Jesus died for you, to take the punishment for your sin; that He came back to life, and that He is still alive today.

C **Consider** the cost of living like God's friend from now on, with Him in charge. It won't be easy. Ask God to help you do this.

D **Do** something about it! In the past you've gone your own way rather than God's way. Will you hand control of your life over to Him from now on? If you're ready to ABCD, then talk to God now. The prayer will help you.

A prayer

Dear God,
I have done and said and thought things that are wrong. I am really sorry. Please forgive me. Thank you for sending Jesus to die for me. From now on, please help me to live as one of Your friends, with You in charge.   Amen

> **Jesus welcomes everyone who comes to Him. If you have put your trust in Him, He has rescued you from your sins and will help you to live for Him. That's great news!**

DAY 13   ...AND UP HE GOT!

Spot the Evidence

Mark has been showing us that **Jesus** has the same authority as **God**. *Unjumble the letters to find what kinds of authority we've seen so far.*

Authority...
- as a CHATEER   T <u>eacher</u>
- over LOPPEE   P <u>eople</u>
- over LIVE RISTIPS   E <u>vil</u>   S <u>pirits</u>
- over KISSNECS   S <u>ickness</u>

But now Jesus claims to have the authority to **forgive sins!**

There are some religious leaders sitting there, and they know that only **God** can forgive sins. They are horrified at Jesus' words! They think this is *blasphemy*—lying about God.

READ
Mark 2v6-12

Answers: Jesus has authority as a teacher, and over people, evil spirits and sickness.

---

xtb   Mark 2v6-12

THINK SPOT

Which one of these is easiest to say?

A Your sins are forgiven.   **B** Get up and walk.

It's easier to say A isn't it?—because no one can <u>see</u> if it's true or not.

So, to show that He <u>does</u> have authority to forgive sins, Jesus also says B!

And what happened? (v12)

Wow! Jesus proved that He has the authority to forgive sins!

THINK+PRAY

Have <u>your</u> sins been forgiven by Jesus?

Thank Him for coming as your Rescuer to forgive your sins.   *Yes*

Not sure   Read *The Servant King* on the previous page again. Ask God to help you understand it.

DAY 14 — THE SIN DOCTOR

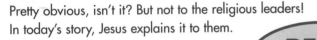

It's not the H E A L T H Y who need a
D O C T E R, but the S I C K o

Pretty obvious, isn't it? But not to the religious leaders!
In today's story, Jesus explains it to them.

READ
Mark 2v13-

Who did Jesus call to follow Him? (v14) LEVI

Levi was a tax collector. He worked for the hated Romans.
The religious leaders were <u>horrified</u> that Jesus made friends with tax
collectors! They thought He should only choose "good" people.

What's that got to do with sick people and doctors?

Follow the lines in the puzzle to find out.

healthy ———— Jesus—the Rescuer

sick ———— people who know they're sinners

doctor ———— people who think they're good
(righteous/respectable)

FLAG CODE

- ◣ = A
- ☰ = C
- ▬ = D
- ▭ = E
- ◻ = H
- ⦿ = I
- ◩ = K
- ◧ = L
- ◺ = O
- ⊞ = R
- ▣ = S
- ◫ = T
- ▨ = Y

Jesus knows that people who are <u>proud</u>
of themselves are unlikely to ask for His
forgiveness.

People who think they're
well don't go to the doctor!

People like the tax collectors came to
Jesus because they knew they <u>needed</u>
forgiveness.

People who know they're sick
go to the doctor for the cure.

**Jesus
is the Sin doctor.**
We're <u>all</u> sinners—
including you and me. But
not everyone thinks they
need Jesus to forgive
them. Do you? Pray
about your answer.

PRAY

FAST FOOD

In today's verses, Jesus says that He is like a **bridegroom**, and that His followers are like **guests** at a wedding.

READ
Mark 2v18-20

What did the people think that Jesus' disciples should be doing? (v18)

F _acting_

> **Did you know?**
>
> **Fasting** means not eating food for a while. It was often a sign of sorrow. In those days many Jews fasted twice a week.

But there was no reason why Jesus' disciples should fast! *Read round the cake to see why not.*

Jesus, the Bridegroom, was with them. It would be like going without food at a wedding!

Jesus, the Son of God, was with His people. It was a time of **joy**, not sorrow!

But what will happen later? (v20)

The bridegroom will be _taken_

Jesus knew that He had come to **die**. At that time, He would be taken away from His followers—and they would be full of sorrow.

But their sorrow would turn to joy when Jesus came back to life again!

Jesus is still alive today! So we have loads of reasons to rejoice!

PRAYER DIARY

Turn to **Rejoicing Reasons** on **page 5** of your **XTB Prayer Diary**. Spend some time praising and thanking God.

DAY 16 NEW FOR OLD

The message about Jesus is that He came to <u>rescue</u> us. He died for us so that we can be friends with God.

That's <u>very different</u> from the set of rules the religious leaders said people had to keep.

The two won't mix! Jesus uses some strange picture language to explain why...

READ
Mark 2v21-22

Sounds odd?
Draw (or write) the pictures Jesus used:

You wouldn't sew a new

onto an old

Or pour new

into old

Rip! If you patch <u>old</u> clothes with <u>new</u> material, they'll *rip*.

Splat! If you pour raw <u>new</u> wine into <u>old</u> brittle wineskins, they'll *split*.

If you try to fit Jesus' message into a human set of rules—it won't work.

- **The Pharisees said:** "you must keep our rules to please God."
- **Jesus says:** "repent and believe the good news." (Mark 1v15)

You can't become a Christian by keeping rules or trying to be good!

That's great news since you can't be totally good all the time.

But if you ***repent*** (turn away from your sins) and ***believe*** the good news about Jesus, then you will be friends with God, and one day live with Him in heaven for ever!

PRAY

Thank God that you don't need to keep a set of rules to be His friend. Thank Him for sending Jesus as your Rescuer.

DAY 17 — CORN ON THE JOB?

In the Old Testament, God made a <u>good</u> rule:
"You shall do no work on the Sabbath." (Exodus 20v10)
One day a week—the Sabbath—was to be a day of **rest**.

But the Pharisees made lots of <u>extra</u> rules. They listed **39** things you mustn't do on the Sabbath!
*Cross out the **X, Y, Z's** to discover three of those things:*

XWYZAXLYKZXIYNZGX — *walking* No more than 1 km from home
YZRXXEAYZPIXYNZXGY — *reaping* Harvesting crops (like corn)
ZCOXYOZZKIXNYZGXY — *cooking* They prepared food the day before

READ
Mark 2v23-28

What did Jesus' disciples do? (v23)

The Pharisees thought this counted as **work** (because they were "reaping" corn!).

But Jesus reminded them of a time when King David had done something similar.
(It's in 1 Samuel 21v1-6.)

Then what did Jesus tell them? (v27-28)

Lord   Sabbath   man

The **S** _abbath_ was made for **m** _an_, not **m** _an_ for the **S** _abbath_.

God's good rule gave people a day of **rest**. But the Pharisees' rules had turned it into a huge **burden**.

The Son of Man is **L** _ord_ even of the Sabbath.

It was <u>God</u> who gave us the Sabbath. But <u>Jesus</u> (sometimes called the Son of Man) is **Lord** of the Sabbath. He's in charge of it—because He is God!

As we'll see tomorrow, the Pharisees <u>hated</u> what Jesus was saying. They wanted to get rid of Him...

PRAY
Today, most Christians have Sunday as their day of rest. It's a great day to meet with other Christians, to help people (as Jesus does in tomorrow's story) and to have a rest doing something you enjoy. Ask God to help you spend your rest day pleasing Him, and enjoying a rest!

DAY 18 HAND IT TO HIM

xtb Mark 3v1-6

Spot the difference. *There are six to find.*

You must keep all of the Sabbath rules.

The Sabbath was made for man not man for the Sabbath.

Yesterday, we saw that God made the Sabbath as a day of **rest**—but the Pharisees filled it with lots of **rules** to keep.

Today, there's another Sabbath argument. Should Jesus <u>heal</u> someone on the Sabbath or not??

READ
Mark 3v1-6

The Pharisees said that you <u>could</u> heal someone on the Sabbath—but only if they were **dying**!

Was this man dying? (v1) **Yes** / **No**

His hand was shrivelled up—but he wasn't dying.
Did Jesus heal him? (v5) **Yes** / **No**

Jesus could have waited until the next day to heal this man— but He didn't! *Fill in the gaps to find out why (v4).*

save
kill
evil
good

Which is lawful on the Sabbath?
—to do **g** good or to do **e** evil
—to **s** save life or to **k** kill

It's always right to do **good** on the Sabbath. So Jesus <u>healed</u> the man.

But the Pharisees were very different. They went out and started to plot **evil**. What did they plot to do? (v6)

THINK + PRAY

What Jesus did was **good** and **right**. But His enemies <u>hated</u> Him for it (and later had Him killed). If you do what's *good* and *right*, you might sometimes be hated or laughed at too. Ask God to help you to do the right thing. Pray that He'll help you to put up with any teasing you get.

DAY 19   SEND IN THE CROWDS

WHO IS JESUS?

The people we meet in Mark's book have different answers to this question:

- Someone to be **killed**? — that's what the Pharisees decided yesterday
- An amazing **healer**? — this is what the crowds think, who flock to Him
- The **Son of God**? — that's what the evil spirits say in today's story
- Someone to **follow**? — this is what tomorrow's verses are about

READ
Mark 3v7-12

Jesus was by Lake Galilee (also called the Sea of Galilee). *Circle it on the map.*

Many people had heard about His amazing miracles. They flocked to see Him. *Find all the places they came from in v8. Draw an arrow from each place to Lake Galilee.*

Who did the evil spirits say Jesus was? (v11)

The B on of god

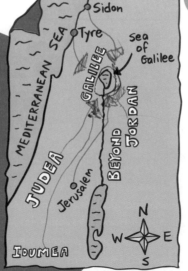

Wow! The evil spirits were right! Jesus **is** the Son of God. *(We've seen loads of evidence for this already in Mark's book.)*

But Jesus wouldn't let them tell the crowds who He was. He knew the people wouldn't understand. They would follow Him for the wrong reasons.

WHO IS JESUS?

Look back at the list at the beginning.
- **Who** do you think Jesus is?
- **Why**? *(Could you explain your reason to someone else?)*

PRAYER DIARY Who could you tell about Jesus this week? _____ Ask God to help you. Write their name on **page 6** of your Prayer Diary.

FOLLOW THE LEADER

Mark
3v13-19

In today's verses, Jesus chooses His 12 closest followers. Can you unjumble their names? (*Some are very unusual!*)

RETEP	Peter
SAMJE	James
NOHJ	John
DANWER	Andrew
LIPPHI	Philip
WEMOLOHTRAB	Bartholomew
THEMWAT	Matthew
SATHOM	Thomas
JEAMS	James
SUEADDAHT	Thaddaeus
NOIMS	Simon
SAJUD	Judas

Check your answers in today's verses.

READ
Mark 3v13-19

Disciple means "pupil" or "student". Jesus had many disciples.
But Jesus chose these twelve to be **Apostles**, which means "sent ones".

What was Jesus going to send them to do? (v14-15)

1 preach
2 drive out demons

From now on, Jesus spent a lot of time with these twelve. He was preparing them to tell others all about Him. Later, after Jesus died and rose again, it would be their job to spread the great news about Him.

Think back over the things we've read about Jesus in Mark's book. (*The pics will remind you of some of them.*)

How would <u>you</u> feel if Jesus chose you to be one of His closest friends?

SUPRISED
And amazed and happy

THINK + PRAY

The wonderful news is that Jesus <u>does</u> want you to be His friend. He loves you. He cares about what happens to you. He loves to listen to you pray. How does that make you feel? Talk to Him about it now.

DAY 21 **THE STORY SO FAR...**

Back in the book of **Genesis**, God made three amazing promises to Abraham. *Crack the code to see them.*

1
L A N D

God promised to give Abraham's family the land of Canaan to live in.

2
C H I L D R E N

God said that Abraham's family would be so HUGE that there would be too many to count!

3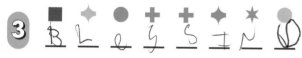
B L E S S I N G

God promised that someone from Abraham's family would be God's way of blessing the whole world.

In this issue of XTB we're going to be reading the book of **Numbers**. It tells us what happened to the Israelites on their journey to the promised land.

They spend most of their time in the desert, so we'll be wondering about their wilderness wanderings!

The story starts on the next page.

700 years later, Abraham's family were known as the Israelites. The book of **Exodus** tells us how they were rescued from Egypt (where they were slaves) and started on their journey to the promised land of Canaan.

SHAPE CODE

A = ■	J = ◆	S = ✚
B = ■	K = ◆	T = ✚
C = ■	L = ◆	U = ✚
D = ■	M = ◆	V = ✚
E = ●	N = ✶	W = ◤
F = ●	O = ★	X = ◤
G = ●	P = ✶	Y = ◥
H = ●	Q = ✶	Z = ◢
I = ◆	R = ★	

COUNTING UP

It's time for a **C E N C U S !**

Moses is the leader of the Israelites. Before they carry on with their journey, God has something for Moses to do.

READ
Numbers 1v1-4

Did You Know?

Abraham's grandson Jacob had thirteen children! (*See pic below.*) The families of his twelve sons were called the twelve **tribes** of Israel.

God told Moses to count up the Israelites. (That's what a **census** is.) But Moses wasn't to count everyone! He didn't include <u>children</u>. And he didn't count any <u>women</u>.

Who **did** Moses count? (v2-3)

20? serve the army MEN (MEN)

Chapter One has a l-o-n-g list of the people who did the counting, and the number in each tribe. At the end, we find out how many men there were in total. The answer is in **verse 46**.

(*In some Bibles, it's at the end of a table of numbers.*)

How many men were there? (v46)

603550

Remember that they only counted the **men**. If you add the women and children there were probably more than **Two Million Israelites!!**

God had kept His promise to Abraham, and given him a H-U-G-E family!

PRAY **God <u>always</u> keeps His promises. Thank Him that He is like this.**

REUBEN · JUDAH · ZEBULUN · DAN · NAPHTALI · ASHER · SIMEON · LEVI · ISACHAR · JOSEPH · BENJAMIN · GAD · DINAH

DAY 22 LORRYLOADS OF LEVIS!

xtb Numbers 1v47-54

True/False Quiz

a) Levi invented jeans. **True / False**

b) Levi was one of Jesus' disciples. **True / False**

c) Levi is my pet walrus. **True / False**

d) Levi was one of Jacob's 12 sons. **True / False**

a) True. Levi Strauss invented the first riveted jeans in 1873.

b) True. This was another Levi. He was a tax collector who became one of Jesus' disciples. *We read about him on Day 14.*

c) 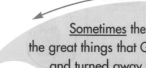 Sadly, not true!

d) True. He's the Levi we're reading about today. Look at the picture of Jacob's sons on the opposite page. Can you spot Levi?

Levi's family (tribe) were known as the **Levites**. When Moses counted up all the Israelites, he <u>didn't</u> count the Levites. *Read the verses to find out why not.*

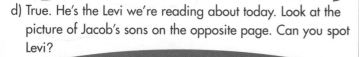

READ
Numbers 1v47-54

Moses had counted all the men who could fight in the army. He didn't count the Levites because they had a *different* job to do. What was it? (v50)

> They were in charge of the
>
> Tabernacle

We'll find out more about this tent (tabernacle) tomorrow.

What do we discover about the Israelites in verse 54?

They did **everything/something/nothing** *God said.*

THINK + PRAY

<u>Sometimes</u> the Israelites forgot the great things that God had done for them, and turned away from Him (as we'll see). But <u>this time</u> they did exactly what He had said.

You and I are like those Israelites. Sometimes we obey God, but sometimes we let Him down. Say sorry to God for the times you disobey Him. Ask Him to help you to live **His** way.

GOD IS WITH US

Take the first letter of each picture to see what the Israelites built.

I A _ _ E R N A _ _ E

God designed it. The Israelites made it. The Levites were in charge of it. But what was it???

Let's jump back to Exodus to find out.

READ
Exodus 25v1-9

The tabernacle was a tent. It looked like this.

Did you know?

The Israelites moved around a lot. So the tabernacle was designed to be easily taken apart. They could pack it up, pick it up and take it with them. Wherever they stopped, the Israelites camped in their tribes round the four sides of the tabernacle. It was in the centre, reminding them that **God was with them all the time.**

Which of these did the Israelites give to make the tabernacle? (v3-7)

Circle your answers.

OLIVE OIL

THINK + PRAY

Read verse 2 again. Only people who really **wanted** to give to God's work did so. Later in Exodus, we find out that they gave so generously that Moses had to stop them! (Exodus 36v5-7) Are <u>you</u> like that? Are you happy to give to God? What can you give Him? Your time? Your money? Your abilities? Pray about your answers.

ARK LARK

Yesterday we found out about the **tabernacle**. Now crack the code to see what was kept *inside* it.

A R K

Did you know?

An **ark** was a box-like container. This means Noah's Ark was actually a HUGE floating box!

The ark inside the tabernacle wasn't a boat! Read the verses to find out what this ark (sometimes called the Covenant Box) was like.

READ
Exodus 25v10-16

Fill in the gaps.

Rings made of
acacia
(v12)

Box covered with
gold
(v11)

Poles covered with
gold
(v13)

Arrow Code

⇧ = A
⇩ = E
 = H
⬆ = I
➡ = K
⬇ = M
 = N
⬅ = O
◁ = R
▷ = S
◁ = T
◁ = Y

What was kept inside the ark?

I ᴛ ʜ ᴇ   T E S T I M O N Y

When God gave the Ten Commandments to Moses, He wrote them on two stone tablets. These are called the **testimony**. They were kept in the ark, which was inside the tabernacle. For this reason, the tabernacle is sometimes called the *Tent of the Testimony*.

Something to treasure!
These two stone tablets held God's special commands to His people. So they were kept safe in this golden ark, like the most valuable treasure.

THINK + PRAY

Something to treasure?
Are God's words <u>special</u> to you? If so, how can you show it? Not by keeping your Bible in a gold box! But by reading it and doing what it says! Do you want to do that? Then ask God to help you!

DAY 25 KEEP A LID ON IT

 Exodus 25v17-22

Yesterday we read about the **ark**. This special box had a special lid.

Take the first letter of each picture to discover two names for this lid.

1 A T O N E M E N T

C O V E R

2 M E R C Y S E A T

We'll find out more about these names after we read about the lid itself...

READ
Exodus 25v17-22

The lid had two cherubim (angels) on it. This lid was like a throne for God.

What did God say He would do there? (v22)

I will m**eet** _____
with you.

But the Israelites couldn't just meet with God! They were sinful (disobedient) people, and their sin got in the way between them and God.

The only way the people could be with God was if He showed them **mercy** (undeserved kindness) and forgave their sins. This is called **atonement**.

THINK + PRAY

Like those Israelites, we <u>all</u> sin. And our sin stops us from being with God. But God showed us **mercy**. He sent Jesus to die on the cross to take the punishment for sin. Jesus paid the price (**atoned**) for our sins, so that we can be forgiven. **Thank God for sending Jesus to die in your place so that you can be forgiven.**

DAY 26 FOLLOW THAT CLOUD!

 Numbers 9v15-23

Now that we've found out about the **tabernacle** and the **ark**, it's time to go back to the book of *Numbers*—where something has settled over the tabernacle...

READ
Numbers 9v15-23

If the cloud was **above** the tabernacle, what must the Israelites do? (v19)

STAY

If the cloud **lifted** from the tabernacle, what must they do? (v21)

GO

God was using the cloud to show the Israelites exactly when to <u>move on</u> and when to <u>stop</u>.

Did the Israelites obey God? (v23) **Yes** / **No**

 THINK SPOT

How does God show <u>you</u> what He wants you to do?

a) With a cloud
b) By email
c) In the Bible

The Israelites would have looked at that cloud every day to check what God wanted them to do. They wouldn't want to miss His instructions.

THINK + PRAY

How often do you read your Bible? How carefully do you follow God's instructions? Do you want to read the Bible more regularly? Do you need to follow God's instructions more carefully? Talk to God about your answers.

TRUMPET CALLS

READ
Numbers 10v1-10

God told Moses to make two **silver trumpets**. They used <u>both</u> to call all of the **Israelites** together, but just <u>one</u> trumpet to call the **leaders**. Short blasts meant it was time to **set out** on their journey. The trumpets were also blown when going out to **battle**, or celebrating **festivals**.

Find all of the blue words in the wordsearch.

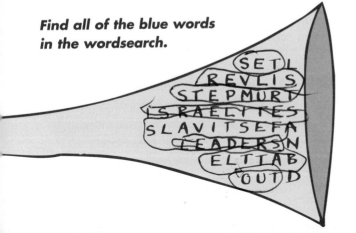

Numbers 10v1-10

Don't be so deafened by the trumpets that you miss the echo of a promise in verse 9!

There are four letters leftover in the wordsearch. What do they spell?

L A N D

God promised to give the Israelites a land of their own. We read about this promise on Day 21.

Now fill in God's words from verse 9.

When you go into battle in your own **L A N D**

...sound a blast on the trumpets. I will rescue you.

God is reminding them that He <u>will</u> keep His promise to give them a land of their own. And He will look after them there.

PRAYER DIARY

God **did** keep His promise to bring the Israelites to the land of Canaan. (You can read about it in Joshua 1v1-6.) Use **page 3** of your **Prayer Diary** to thank God that He <u>always</u> keeps His promises.

DAY 28 GOODBYE TO SINAI

Which of these would you take on holiday with you?

The Israelites have been camped at Mount Sinai for nearly a year. But now the cloud lifts from above the tabernacle, and it's time to set off. But not on holiday! It's time to go to the land God has promised them.

READ
Numbers 10v11-13

Whose command were they following? (v13)

M o s e s

God was leading them to the land of Canaan, just as He had promised.

Verses 14-28 tell us the order they all travelled in. The tribes followed each other in order—a bit like a school trip, where each class walks with their teacher.

READ
Numbers 10v33-36

What went ahead of the Israelites? (v33)

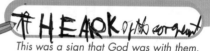
THE ARK of the covenant

This was a sign that God was with them.

Fill in the gaps in Moses' words.

Arise, O Lord v35

Return **O Lord** v36

Moses **knew** God was with them. They had a long way to go, but he was **sure** God would bring them safely to Canaan. *That's why (in v29) he invited his brother-in-law to come with them.*

THINK + PRAY

Are you as confident as Moses? Or do you sometimes worry about the future? Talk to God about anything you're worried about. Ask Him to help you to trust Him.

How many words can you make with these letters? *You can use each letter as many times as you want.*

A B H E T R

Heart ~~mat~~
BATH HAT
BAT RAT
TABERAH
teeth

Here's one ~~I guess you didn't make!~~ → TABERAH

Taberah means "burning". Find out in today's reading why the Israelites call their next stop Taberah.

READ
Numbers 11v1-3

Moan, moan, moan... The Israelites were experts at complaining! So God taught them two important lessons.

Cross out all the MOANs to find them.

**GOMOANDHEMOANAR
SUSMOANCOMPMOAN
LAINMOANING**

GOD HEARS US COMPLAINING

Would you be ashamed of moaning if you remembered that **God** is listening? He gives us everything we have—our food, our homes, our friends, our possessions—EVERYTHING!

But often, instead of saying thank you, we just moan about them!

**GMOANODISAMOANN
GRYMOANATCOMOAN
MPLAIMOANNING**

GOD IS ANGRY AT COMPLAINING

God showed His anger by sending f~~ire~~ to the Israelite camp. (v1) *That's why they called it Taberah.*

PRAY

Moses needed to ask God to forgive the Israelites (v2). Think of some of the ways you've been moaning recently. Say sorry to God and ask Him to help you not to be a moaner.

DAY 30 MIND YOUR MANNAS

God had done some **wonderful** things for the Israelites.

- Rescued them from slavery in _Egypt_
- _promised_ to be with them.
- Promised to give them a _land_ of their own.
- Given them _food_ (called _manna_) every day.

Use these words to fill in the gaps.

Promised · manna · food · land · Egypt

You can read about manna in Exodus 16.

But look how the Israelites felt about it...

Oh no - not manna again!

It's manna for breakfast, manna for lunch and manna for tea.

I'm fed up with manna. I want meat!

Do you remember the great food we had in Egypt?

Cucumbers! Fish! Melons! Onions!

And it was FREE!

What an ungrateful lot!

READ
Numbers 11v4-10

How did God feel about their moaning? (v10)

He was _angry_

More about God's reaction tomorrow.

PRAY
Our food doesn't fall with the dew at night! But it does come from God. Thank God for the food that He gives you, and for the people who cook it. *Say a big thank you to them today!*

DAY 31 MORE MOANING

Yesterday, we read about the Israelites' moaning. What were they complaining about?

a) The price of airline tickets.
b) Crusts on their cucumber sandwiches.
c) Eating manna every day.

Now, it's Moses' turn. He's in a moaning mood too!
Take the first letter of each picture to see what he's complaining about.

Why have you brought this

T R O U B L E

on me?

Where can I get

M E A T

for all these people?

They keep

W A I L I N G

about meat!

It's all too

M U C H

for me!

 THINK SPOT Was Moses right to grumble at God? How do you think God will respond? *Read the verses to find out.*

READ
Numbers 11v10-17

Even though Moses was grumbling at God, God was **kind** to him. What did God give Moses to help him? (v16-17)

70 L E A D E R S

These leaders would help Moses, so that he didn't have to do everything himself.

THINK + PRAY Did you know that you can be completely honest with God? If you're worried, upset or fed up— you can tell Him! Moaning is never right (as we saw on day 29), but we can always tell God the <u>truth</u> about how we feel. Talk to Him now about how you're feeling—and thank Him that you can be honest with Him.

DAY 32 MISSION IMPOSSIBLE?

xtb Numbers 11v18-23

We were better off in Egypt!

How insulting! What was it <u>really</u> like in Egypt?

work Egyptian badly slaves

The Israelites had been s<u>laves</u> in Egypt. They were forced to do back-breaking **w** <u>ork</u> for their **E** <u>gyptian</u> slave masters, who treated them really **b** <u>adly</u>.

God had shown great kindness by rescuing the Israelites—but they just moaned about meat! Now Moses told them to purify (or consecrate) themselves to be ready for what God would do...

READ Numbers 11v18-20

You will eat meat until you're sick of it! (v20)

Was God going to give them meat? **Yes / No**

How long for? (v20)

For <u>a month</u>

But Moses couldn't work out where all the meat would come from...

READ Numbers 11v21-23

Moses seemed to have forgotten that God had already been raining manna on them for a year!

Is the LORD's arm too short? (v23)

A **short arm** wouldn't be able to do much! But **God** isn't like that—as Moses will soon find out!

Read round the spirals to see what God is like.

With God all things are possible. Matthew 19v26

Nothing is impossible with God. Luke 1v37

PRAY Thank God that nothing is impossible for Him.

DAY 33 HOLY HELPER

In the Old Testament, God gave His Spirit to <u>selected</u> people who had <u>special</u> jobs. *Follow the lines to see some of them.*

Gideon

Bezalel

Samson

Artistic skills to make the tabernacle. (Exodus 31v1-5)

Superhuman strength. (Judges 14v6)

Ability to lead God's people to victory. (Judges 6v34)

Moses had God's Holy Spirit. Do you remember how God promised to give Moses 70 men to help him lead the Israelites? (Day 31) They too needed the Holy Spirit to help them serve God.

Did You Know?

The Holy Spirit isn't a force—like electricity! He's a person. He's God!

READ
Numbers 11v24-25

When the 70 men were given God's Spirit, they began to **prophesy** (to speak God's message). But two men weren't prophesying in the same place as the others. So Joshua wanted to stop them...

READ
Numbers 11v26-30

What did Moses say to Joshua? (v29)

Spirit all Lord

I wish that the **L** _Lord_ would give His **S** _pirit_ to **a** _ll_ His people!

THINK SPOT

In the Old Testament, God gave His Spirit to **selected** people. But in the New Testament, God gives the Holy Spirit to **all** believers. (*This first happened on the Day of Pentecost—Acts 2v1-4.*)

PRAYER DIARY

If you are a Christian, God has given <u>you</u> His Spirit too, to help you to serve God and live His way. Thank God for the amazing gift of His Spirit to help you to live for Him. *Find out more on **Page 7** of your **Prayer Diary**.*

DAY 34 THREE FAB FACTS

1 ◁ ← ▽ ↘

God keeps His W O R D

What had God promised to send the Israelites?

a) Cucumbers
b) Pumpkins
c) Meat

In today's reading, God keeps His word to send them meat.

READ
Numbers 11v31-32

ARROW CODE

D = ↘
E = ⇓
F = ↗   L = ➘   R = ◁
N = ↙   S = ▷
O = ←   U = ▽
H = ↗   P = ↖   W = ◁
I = ⬆

2 ↖ ← ◁ ⇓ ▽ ↗ ▽ ↘

God is P O W E R F U L

God sent oodles of **Q** _quail_ (small birds) to land all round the Israelite camp. The quail were piled nearly a metre high!

That's like standing in a snowdrift right up to your chest!

What an amazing answer to God's promise!

But God was <u>angry</u> with the Israelites...

READ
Numbers 11v33-35

3 P U N I S H E S
↖ ▽ ↖ ⬆ ▷ ↖ ⇓ ▷

God ~~P U N Y~~ _ _ _ _ **sin**

The Israelites had moaned about God's good gift of *manna* to eat. So He punished them with a terrible plague.

God is just as **powerful** today, and He still **punishes** sin. But long before the time of Moses He had made a promise to send a *Rescuer* to save His people. He kept His **word** by sending *Jesus* to die on the cross. Jesus took the punishment that we deserve, so that <u>we</u> can be forgiven.

PRAY Thank God for keeping His promise to send Jesus as Rescuer, to save those who believe in Him.

DAY 35 MOANALOTS!

"I hate school. It's so boring!"

"My friends stay up <u>much</u> later than me. It's not fair!"

"Do I <u>have</u> to wash up? I did it yesterday!"

"I want a TV in my room. Everyone else has one!"

 Moaning Mona

 Grumbling Gary

 Sulking Susan

 Wailing William

These four are just like the Israelites, aren't they? They're all **moanalots!** Two of them are Christians —but sadly you can't tell which two!

Crack the code to see what they <u>should</u> be like.

Be _ _ _ _ _ _ _ _

in all circumstances.

This is what Paul says we should be like. Read about it in his letter to Christians in Thessalonica (in Greece).

READ
1 Thessalonians 5v16-18

= A
= F
= H
= K
= L
= N
= T
= U

What do you think it means to be thankful in all circumstances?

a) give thanks when things are going well
b) gives thanks when God gives us something
c) give thanks all the time, no matter how things are
d) give thanks when God answers our prayers

God had done some **amazing** things for the Israelites, (*can you remember some?*), but all <u>they</u> did was MOAN!

Are <u>you</u> a moanalot like them? Or are you thankful to God for the great things He's given you?

Jot down some things to thank God for.

PRAY Now **thank** God for each one—and ask Him to help you not to be a moanalot!

The Book of Ephesians

 Do you like getting letters? I love it! As soon as the postman arrives I stop what I'm doing and rush to see if anything exciting has arrived!

Crack the code to see who this letter is for and who sent it.

A   **E**   **H**   **L**   **P**   **S**   **U**

To: *Christians living in* _____

From: __ __ __ __ __

But we can read it too!
It's in the Bible, and it's called **Ephesians**.

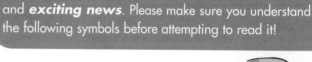

Warning! Ephesians is a letter packed full of **BIG IDEAS** and *exciting news*. Please make sure you understand the following symbols before attempting to read it!

  Put on your imaginary seat belt for high-speed journeys through time and space.

 Stop and learn a great new word.

 Check you remember what this word means? Go to Day 36 to remind yourself.

 This is a **BIG** idea. Read this bit again, and say the word *"Wow!"* out loud five times.

 Great! Let's get started!
Go straight on to Day 36.

DAY 36 **1, 2, 3, GO!**
CONTINUED

Paul

Ephesians 1v1-3

READ
Ephesians 1v1

What's special about Paul? (v1)

He's an **a**_____

An apostle is someone who was chosen by God and sent to teach us the truth about Jesus. We should listen to what he says!

Who's Paul writing to? (v1)

_____ in Ephesus.

Your Bible may say **saints**. That doesn't mean extra-special people. It means everyone who believes in Jesus!

READ
Ephesians 1v2

Your Bible may have used our first special word: **GRACE**.

Read around the present to see what GRACE means.

God's HUGE kindness to people who don't deserve it.

Circle the things that make you excited. Add some of your own.

Christmas

Parties

Birthdays

Chocolate

Holidays

READ
Ephesians 1v3

...to see why Paul's so excited!

Underline the correct words

Paul's **cross with/thanking and praising** God for giving us EVERY spiritual **banana/blessing** because of **our good behaviour/Jesus**.

No wonder Paul's excited! Spiritual blessings are the good things God gives us because of Jesus. *More about exactly what these blessings are in the next few days.*

PRAYER DIARY

GO! It's your turn to praise God! Fill in blanks 1-3 on **pages 8 + 9** of your Prayer Diary and pray up to the first ☺.

DAY 37 CHOSEN CHILDREN

xtb Ephesians 1v4-6

Have you ever been chosen to...

I choose you

☐ answer a question
☐ play in a team
☐ be in a play

If you're a Christian you've been chosen for something very special. This choice was made a <u>long</u> time ago!

READ
Ephesians 1v4-6

Who chose us and when? (v4)

_____ chose us **before** _____

_____

What did God choose us to be? (v5)

His _____

Cleaners   Children   Gardeners

WOW! Did you know God chose you to be His child before the world was made?

Why did God choose us? (v5, 6)

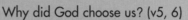

Draw a 😊 by the 2 right answers.

○ It pleased Him, He wanted to.
○ Because we're great.
○ To bring Him praise.

He didn't choose us because we are really nice or good—but because He **wanted** to.

How did God make us His children? (v5)

Through **J**_____.

Being God's child is one of the amazing spiritual blessings we have because of Jesus!

PRAYER DIARY

Fill in blanks 4-5 in your **Prayer Diary** (page 9) and pray up to the second 😊.

DAY 38 FREE AND FORGIVEN

We're in the slave market and we want to set free two slaves. How much will it cost to set them free?

PRICE LIST...
△ = £50
● = £30
■ = £70

But how much did **God** pay to set <u>us</u> free?
Read the verses to find out.

READ
Ephesians 1v7-8

Did You Know?

Redeem / Redemption
Means to pay a price to set someone free.
Your Bible may use these words in v7.

Paul says we've been **set free**.
What does he mean? (v7)

Our **s**_____ are **f**_____

Sin is doing what **we** want instead of what **God** wants. Sin traps us and separates us from God. It's just like we are <u>slaves</u> and need to be <u>set free</u> (or redeemed).

Use the code to see what price Jesus paid to set us free from sin.

L	B	O	D
1	2	3	4

2 1 3 3 4
His __ __ __ __ __

Jesus set us free by dying on the cross! WOW! That's a huge price to pay!

Why did God free us? (v7)
☐ We deserved it
☐ His grace and kindness 36

*Check out Day 36 to see what **grace** means.*

Circle the words that describe **God's grace**. (v7, 8)

Stingy
HUGE   **GENEROUS**
Tiny

PRAYER DIARY

Join Paul in praising God. Fill in blanks 6-7 on **Page 9** of your **Prayer Diary**. Pray up to the third ☺.

DAY 39 A GRAND PLAN

Colour in the dotted shapes to see who God's plans are all about!

God chose us and set us free through **Jesus**. But that's not all!

We're going forward to the end of time when Jesus comes again!

READ
Ephesians 1v9-10

God wants **you** to know His plans!

What is God's plan? (v10)

Cross out the wrong words.

> To bring **some things/everything** in heaven **and/or** earth together with **us/Jesus** in the centre, in charge.

 Ephesians 1v9-10

What spoils our world?

Unjumble the letters

__ __ __

Sin spoils our world. People ignore God and do what they want! God plans to make a **new world**. There'll be no sin, and Jesus will be at the centre, in charge!

Read around the world to see what God's plans are like.

God's plans always happen!

What a great ending to God's rescue plan! Jesus in charge over a whole new world!

PRAYER DIARY

Fill in blank 8 on **Page 9** of your **Prayer Diary** and pray up to the 4th 😊.

Who can be sure of receiving the good things God gives through Jesus?

 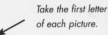

Take the first letter of each picture.

_ _ _

_ _ _ _ _ _ _ _ _ _ _

READ
Ephesians 1v11-12

In v11-12 Paul's talking about **Jews** (God's Old Testament people).

Why did God choose some Jews to follow Jesus? (v11, 12)

☐ They're clever
☐ He planned it
☐ They're good
☐ For His praise

T = *true*
F = *false*

Everyone who wasn't a Jew was called a **Gentile**. God also chose some Gentiles to believe.

READ
Ephesians 1v13-14

Put these events in order by numbering the boxes **1**, **2** *and* **3**. *(v13)*

☐ Given the Holy Spirit
☐ Heard about Jesus
☐ Believed

Both Jews <u>and</u> Gentiles can receive God's blessings through **Jesus**. It's all part of God's plan to bring Him praise.

Who <u>guarantees</u> (makes us sure) that we'll receive God's promises? (v14)

The _ _ _ _

_ _ _ _ _ _ _ _

God gives all Christians the Holy Spirit to show we belong to Him and to keep us going until we're with God in heaven.

PRAYER DIARY

Fill in blanks 9-11 in your **Prayer Diary** (page 9) and pray up to the final 🙂 .

MORE TO EXPLORE

We've explored from before creation to the end of time!

Use the explorer's map to see what we've discovered.

God has given us **E** _ _ _ _ _ _ spiritual

blessing because of _ _ _ _ _ _ .

If God's already given us every spiritual blessing, what should we pray for?

READ
Ephesians 1v15-19

What does Paul want the Holy Spirit to give the Ephesians? (v17)

W_____ and **R**_____

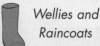 *Wellies and Raincoats*

 Wisdom and Revelation

EXPLORER'S MAP

This means that Paul wants the Holy Spirit to help us <u>see</u> and <u>understand</u> something more clearly.

Use the map to find out what!

The _ _ _ _ _ things we have

through _ _ _ _ _ _ _ .

Write down two things to understand and enjoy more.

1.The **h**_____
Christians have (v18)

We can be sure God's great plan will happen and He'll keep all His promises.

2.God' **p**_____ (v19)

We can rely on God's power to help us follow Jesus.

PRAY

Dear God, help me to explore and understand the good things I have through Jesus more and more. Amen.

DAY 42 POWER TRIP

xtb Ephesians 1v19-23

Paul's praising God again!
*Cross out the **X**, **Y**, and **Z**s to see what for.*

XHIYSPZYOWXXYZEZXYZR

 Paul's taking us on a trip to heaven to see the **power** God the Father has given Jesus.

READ
Ephesians 1v19-23

How did God show how **great** His power is? (v19, 20)

He **r**_____ Jesus from the **d**_____.

Remember—God uses that power to help us follow Him! WOW!

Now Jesus is at God's right hand—the most important place of all!

What does Jesus rule over? (v22)
Some things / Everything

Write **Jesus** in the crown to show that He rules over <u>all</u> other powers.

Angels   Evil spirits
Human rulers

Who does Jesus use His power to help? (v22)

THE _ _ U R _ _

C H
C H

Did you realise how important God's people are to Him? Powerful King Jesus is looking after His people (the church) and using us in His plans!

PRAY   **Praise God for the power He's given Jesus.**

DAY 43 BEFORE...

Draw lines to the correct pictures.

Before a haircut
Before a bath
Before dinner
Before a bike ride
Before a party

Today Paul reminds the Ephesians what they were like <u>before</u> they followed Jesus.

READ
Ephesians 2v1-3

What were they before they followed Jesus? (v1) **D**_____

They weren't physically dead!
—but they were separated from God and the eternal life He gives.

Which ways did they follow? (v2)
Tick the 2 correct signs. ☑

The World's Way
God's Way
The Devil's Way

Who did they please? (v3)
☐ God
☐ Themselves

Put a cross in the box next to God's Way   ☒

xtb   Ephesians 2v1-3

Before people follow Jesus they <u>don't</u> go God's way. They please themselves, follow everyone else and go the way the devil wants.

How does Paul describe them at the end of v3?

☐ God's friends
☐ God's enemies facing His anger

What a terrible situation they were in!
Get the good news tomorrow!

PRAYER DIARY

Pray for someone you know who isn't a Christian using Page 10 of your Prayer Diary.

DAY 44 AMAZING GRACE

Remember the terrible situation the Ephesians were in?

Read along the smile to see what changed everything.

God's _ _ _ _ _ _ **and** _ _ _ _ _ _

 MERCY: God's decision to help us and not treat us the way we deserve.

 GRACE: See Day 36.

mercygrace

READ
Ephesians 2v4-10

*It's a l-o-n-g reading. Look out for **mercy** and **grace** as you read it.*

What has God done through Jesus?

v5 Made us **a**_____

v6 Raised us to be with **J**_____

AND verse 7 says God uses <u>us</u> to show the universe how wonderful He is!

 WoW!

Use the red letters to discover what way the Ephesians are going now. (v10)

What a huge change! God saved them from their terrible situation and helped them go <u>His</u> way and do great things for Him!

Why does God save us? (v4-5, v8-9)
Because of...

☐ Our good works—we deserve it.

☐ His mercy, grace and love.

Who's saying the right thing? (v9)

I'm a Christian—I'm so wonderful!
God is wonderful!

PRAY

It's <u>God</u> who deserves the praise! If you are a Christian, thank Him for saving you.

WALLBREAKER, PEACEMAKER

 xtb Ephesians 2v14-18

Crack the code to see who the wall separates.

_ _ _ _ | _ _ _ _ _ _ _

Wall Code

D · E
G · I
J
N · L
R · O
S
T · V
W
· Y

Jews: God's Old Testament people

Gentiles: Everyone else

Keeping God's law made Jews different from Gentiles. God wanted the Jews to teach Gentiles about Him. Instead they hated each other! It was like there was a wall between them!

READ
Ephesians 2v14-18

Who brought peace between Jews and Gentiles? (v14, 15)

J

<u>*Finish the picture*</u> to show Jesus creating one new group out of two enemy groups (v14).

Gentiles

Jews

*God's New People Jews **and** Gentiles*

That's not the only wall Jesus broke down. Who does this wall separate?

_ _ _ _ _ _ _ | _ _ _

Sin (*doing what we want and disobeying God's law*) separates Jews <u>and</u> Gentiles from God. They <u>both</u> need Jesus to bring them peace with God.

How did Jesus bring peace? (v16)

By dying on the c_____

Because Jesus died, Jews and Gentiles can be together with God! (v18) The wall's broken!

 WOW!

PRAY

Read v18 again. You can go into God's presence and talk to Him anytime because Jesus died for you! Thank God for this.

DAY 46 **YOU BELONG**

Paul wants the Gentiles (non-Jews) in Ephesus to be **sure** they're members of God's new people.

READ
Ephesians 2v19-22

What had the Gentiles been like? (v19)

F_____

They were so cut off from God's people they were like foreigners!

How does Paul describe them now? (v19)
Draw a 😊 *by the right answers.*

⬤ Part of God's family (household)

⬤ Still foreigners

⬤ Citizens of God's kingdom

Once strangers, now part of the family!

Find the letters in the family portrait to discover what made the difference.

_ _ _ _ _

Everyone who believes in Jesus is part of God's amazing family that stretches round the world!

How does Paul describe God's people? (v21-22) ✔

 We're like a building where the Holy Spirit lives!

How does Paul describe Jesus? (v20)

The _____ stone

The cornerstone! The most important stone! Without Jesus God's people would fall apart!

If you follow Jesus, you're like a brick in God's building.

Write your name in the brick!

PRAY

Thank God that Jesus makes us part of God's new people.

DAY 47 GRACE AT WORK

What would you like to be when you grow up?

Follow the arrows to find out about **Paul's** amazing job.

36 GRACE AND HIS
ABOUT → TO TELL
GOD'S → GENTILES
SECRET PLAN! ←

What secret plan?

Read the verses to find out.

READ
Ephesians 3v1-7

What is God's secret plan (mystery)? (v6)

God's   Gentiles
Jews   Jesus

G_____ can be part of **G**_____ people
as well as **J**_____ because **J**_____ died.

How did the apostle Paul know God's secret? (v5) ✔
☐ He's very clever
☐ The Holy Spirit revealed it to him

God kept some of His plan secret until Jesus died and rose again. Then the Holy Spirit showed it to people like Paul.

Tick two **true** statements about Paul's great job. (v7)
☐ Paul deserved it
☐ It was a gift from God because of His grace
☐ God gave Paul the power to do it

Loads of grace! The Gentiles are part of God's family and God is helping Paul to tell them!

THINK + PRAY Grace is God's HUGE kindness to people who don't deserve it. People like you and me! Thank God for His grace!

DAY 48 PART OF A PLAN

Read around the church to remind yourself about God's big plan.

To bring everything together under Jesus' rule, with Him in charge.

God's people, (called the church), are part of that plan!

READ
Ephesians 3v8-13

Gentiles are becoming part of God's people just like God planned! Who does Paul want to tell? (v9)

All people / Some people / No people

Why did God bring Jews and Gentiles together in His church? (v10)   *Take the first letter of each picture.*

To make known His _ _ _ _ _ _ _

Look at the picture of the church. It's full of different people! Circle someone younger than you, someone older, and someone with different colour skin.

God makes all sorts of different people friends through Jesus. People who wouldn't normally be friends! God uses His people, the church, to show how wise He is and to show that His plan is happening. WOW!

Why might the Ephesians be discouraged? (v13)
- ☐ Their football team is losing
- ☐ Paul is suffering in prison

But they don't need to worry! God's in charge and He's got a great plan!

THINK + PRAY

Are there other Christians you find it hard to be friends with? It's important that Christians love each other. Ask God to help you to love other Christians, even when it's hard.

DAY 49 GET PRAYING!

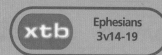
READ
Ephesians 3v14-19

POWERHOUSE

PROMISING

PATHETIC

PUNY

How strong are you?
Shade up to level that describes you.

What sort of strength does Paul want the Spirit to give Christians? (v16)

Underline the answer.

BIG MUSCLES

STRENGTH INSIDE, IN OUR HEARTS

Who lives in our hearts to make them strong? (v17)

O L

V E

Paul wants us to understand

how **BIG** Jesus' ＿ ＿ ＿ ＿ is. (v18, 19)

We've found out lots about Jesus' love as we've explored Ephesians. *Find these words in the wordsearch:*
chosen, forgiven, mercy, grace, set free.

Some are backwards!

```
    M   O
  G R A C E
E E R F T E S
R F O R G I V E N
N E S O H C E
  M E R C Y
```

But we need God's help to find out ＿ ＿ ＿ ＿

Use the leftover letters (in order)

Jesus' love is so large there's always more to explore!

PRAY

It's not easy being a Christian! We need help to live God's way. Pray that Jesus will live in your heart forever and make you strong.

PRAY

Pray that God will help you understand and enjoy Jesus' love more and more.

DAY 50 · A GLORIOUS ENDING

Circle the things you **can't** do.

 Tie shoelaces

 Handstands

Fly helicopters

Swim

Live on the moon

Paul praises God because there's **nothing** God can't do.

READ
Ephesians 3v20-21

What does Paul believe God can do? (v20, 21)

✔ *Tick the two right answers.*

☐ Bits of what he's asked for
☐ Exactly what he asked
☐ More than he asked
☐ More than he can imagine asking

 WOW! Paul knows that God will do more for the Ephesians than he can even <u>think</u> of asking!

Use the first letter of each picture to complete the speech bubble.

God is _ _ _ _ _ !

God's does _ _ _ _ _ things!

How long should we bring glory and praise to God! (v21)

For

Have you found Ephesians hard? Well done for getting this far!

 PRAYER DIARY

CONGRATULATIONS!
You've successfully explored Ephesians 1-3!
Your final task is to explore the prayer on **Page 11** of your **Prayer Diary**.

I live near London in **England**—but would love to live in Sydney in **Australia**. It's a beautiful city and I have good friends there.

I have other friends who are moving to **France** because they want more sunshine!

If you could live in another country, which would you choose?

The Israelites were moving to a new country. But they weren't chasing after friends or sunshine. They had been promised their own land—a good land—by **God!**

FLAG CODE

	= A
	= B
	= C
	= D
	= E
	= G
	= H
	= I
	= L
	= N
	= R
	= S

In fact, God had made **three** amazing promises to the Israelites...

God promised to give the Israelites the land of Canaan to live in.

God said that the Israelite nation would be so HUGE that there would be too many to count!

God promised that someone from the Israelite nation would be God's way of blessing the whole world.

The Bible tells us how God keeps these promises.
Flick over to the next page to check out the story so far.

PAST, PRESENT AND FUTURE

Numbers 1v46
Exodus 3v7-8

PAST: Children

At the beginning of **Numbers**, God told Moses to count the Israelites.

Moses counted all the men who were old enough to fight in the army.

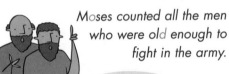

READ
Numbers 1v46

How many men were there?

> **6**

Over 600 thousand men! If you add the women and children, there were probably over **Two Million Israelites!!**

*God had certainly kept His promise to make them a **HUGE** nation!*

PRESENT: Land

In **Exodus**, God spoke to Moses from a burning bush. *Jump back to Exodus to see what God told Moses about the promised land of Canaan.*

READ
Exodus 3v7-8

What was their new land going to be like?

In **Numbers** we see how God is keeping His promise to bring the Israelites to Canaan. They're on their way, following God's special cloud.

FUTURE: Blessing

The Israelites were a huge nation, and on their way to Canaan. But the **third** promise hadn't happened yet. It was well over 1000 years in the future!

They would have to trust Him to keep that promise too.

Shh! Secret!

We know something the Israelites don't know! We know how God kept that third promise.

Copy all the red letters from this page.

— — — — — — — — —

More about that soon

PRAY Thank God for sending **Jesus** as His way of blessing the whole world.

DAY 52 **I SPY...**

The Israelites have reached Paran, which is very close to Canaan. Now God repeats His promise to give them the land.

READ
Numbers 13v1-2

Choose some men to
e_____ the land of
C_____, which
I am **g**_____ to
the Israelites. (v2)

Moses chose **twelve spies** to check out the land. (*They're listed in v3-16.*)

READ
Numbers 13v17-20

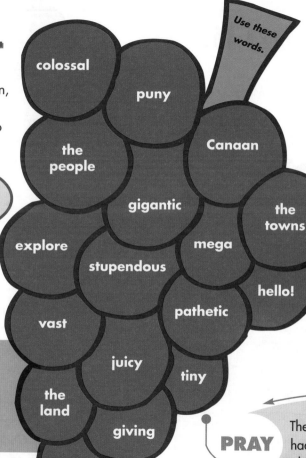

Use these words.

colossal

puny

the people

Canaan

gigantic

the towns

explore

mega

stupendous

hello!

vast

pathetic

juicy

tiny

the land

giving

heavy

List three things the spies had to find out about:

1 The _____

2 The _____

3 The _____

God had promised them a **good** land, full of fab food...

READ
Numbers 13v23

Find some words to describe those huge grapes.

PRAY The land was just as **good** as God had promised. Thank God that He <u>always</u> keeps His promises.

The spies also spotted some very BIG people! *More about them tomorrow...*

WE CAN DO IT!

xtb — Numbers 13v25-33

The Israelites had nearly reached Canaan. So Moses sent **twelve spies** to check out the land...

Find out how strong the people are.

Check out their towns too.

And see what the land is like.

Bring back some fruit if you can.

So the 12 spies went into Canaan.

The land was fabulous!

Let's take these grapes

But the cities were strong...

...and the people were tall!

So 10 spies gave a **bad** report.

They're too strong for us!

We even saw giants!

But Joshua and Caleb didn't agree. They **trusted** God.

We can do it!

Based on Numbers 13v17-33

READ
Numbers 13v30-33

*The Israelites had to choose who to **trust**.*

Will they trust **God?**
- King of the Universe
- Rescued them from Egypt
- Provides food for them every day in the desert

Or...
Will they trust **10 men?**
- Ten ordinary blokes
- Not kings of anything
- Can't do miracles

Who do you think the Israelites will trust?

THINK SPOT

Imagine that you were there. Who do you think you would have trusted? Why?

PRAY

Think of at least three reasons why you can trust God. Deuteronomy 31v6 says, "The LORD will not fail you or abandon you." Thank God that He is like this.

DAY 54 TRUE OR FALSE?

After the 12 spies came back from Canaan, this is what the people decided.

Let's choose a leader and go back to Egypt.

Put True or False by these possible reasons for saying this:

a) The Israelites didn't have a leader. **True / False**

b) Canaan would be a bad place to live. **True / False**

c) They'd had a good life in Egypt. **True / False**

Now check your answers:

a) *False:* **Moses** was their leader, and **God** was their King!

b) *False:* Canaan was **good** land, as God has promised.

c) *False:* They had been badly treated **slaves** in Egypt!

So why did the people say this?

Read round their faces.

They believed the bad report from the 10 spies instead of trusting God.

Re-read the cartoon on the opposite page. Then read the next part of the story.

READ
Numbers 14v1-10

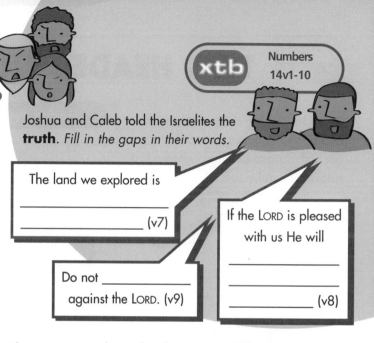

xtb Numbers 14v1-10

Joshua and Caleb told the Israelites the **truth**. *Fill in the gaps in their words.*

The land we explored is _____ _____ (v7)

If the LORD is pleased with us He will _____ _____ _____ (v8)

Do not _____ against the LORD. (v9)

This was great advice—but the Israelites didn't listen! What were they planning to do? (v10)

S_____ them.

We'll find out what happened tomorrow...

PRAYER DIARY

The Bible tells us that we can <u>always</u> trust God. *Turn to* **Page 12** *of your* **Prayer Diary** *to find out more.*

DAY 55 TWO HEADED COIN

Today we see two sides of God's character. They seem quite different, but both have to be there—like the two sides of the same coin...

Mercy
God is merciful.

Justice
God is just.

Mercy
To show someone kindness that they don't deserve.

Justice
Making sure that sin is punished and good is rewarded.

God is Merciful

Even though the Israelites had **moaned** so much, God had brought them safely across the desert to the edge of Canaan.

But the people in Canaan were tall and strong, so the Israelites were **afraid**. They didn't _trust_ God —and threatened to kill Joshua and Caleb!

God is Just

God was angry with the Israelites. He said He would punish their sin by destroying them all, as they deserved.

But Moses begged Him not to...

READ
Numbers 14v13-16

The Israelites <u>deserved</u> to be punished, but Moses worried about what the other nations would think of God.

> The **n**_____ will say that you **k**_____ your people in the desert because you were not **a**_____ to bring them into the land you **p**_____ them. (v16)

promised   nations   able   killed

God is Merciful

So God forgave the Israelites...

READ
Numbers 14v20

God is Just

Because God is **merciful**, He didn't destroy the Israelites. But because He is **just**, He had to punish their sin. So He told them they would NOT go into Canaan. Instead they would spend another <u>40 years</u> in the desert. (v21-38)

More tomorrow...

THINK+PRAY

God is Just
<u>Everyone</u> sins. Because God is just, He must punish that sin.

God is Merciful
God sent **Jesus** to take the punishment <u>we</u> deserve, so that we can be forgiven.

God is both just and merciful. Thank Hi

DAY 56 — TOO LATE TO TURN BACK!

 Numbers 14v39-45

Did you find yesterday's story hard to understand? The Israelites did! They didn't get it at all!

The story so far

Because God is **merciful**, He didn't destroy the Israelites. But because He is **just**, He did punish their sin. They were to spend the next 40 years in the desert.

During that time, everyone who <u>hadn't</u> trusted God would die. Only the few who trusted Him—like Joshua and Caleb—would live to go to Canaan.

The Israelites didn't like the sound of that! So they changed their minds about going into the promised land...

> We have sinned! We'll go to the land God promised.

But it was too late...

Take the first letter of each picture to find out what Moses told them.

> Why are you
>
> _ _ _ _ _ _ _ _ _ _ _ _ _
>
> the LORD's command? You won't succeed!

> Don't go. The _ _ _ _ is not with you. Your enemies will defeat you.

Read the verses to see what happened.

READ
Numbers 14v39-45

Circle the correct answers.

The Israelites headed for the **hill/valley/river** country. But **Mark/Moses/Miriam** didn't go with them, and the **park/ark/aardvark** stayed in the camp. Then their enemies **ignored/attacked/danced with** them, and beat them!

THINK SPOT
The people were finally obeying God's original command. But only because they didn't like His new instructions! They were <u>still</u> doing what **they** thought was best instead of obeying **God**.

THINK+PRAY

What about <u>you</u>? Do you need to say sorry to God for doing what <u>you</u> think is best instead of obeying <u>Him</u>? Or do you need to ask His help to **trust** Him more? Talk to Him about your answers.

DAY 57 SOGGY SAGA

Do you remember the two-sided coin?

Mercy — God is merciful.
Justice — God is just.

Check what Mercy and Justice mean on Day 55.

In the next two days we'll see __both__ sides of God's character again.

But first, **number these events** in the correct order (1–4).

The Israelites **grumbled** about God's miracle food, manna.
YUK!

God sent **ten plagues** to rescue the Israelites from Egypt

The Israelites didn't go to Canaan because they **didn't trust** God.

God provided **daily food** — manna — in the desert.

Did you notice how __good__ God has been to the Israelites? And how often they've turned their backs on Him?!

Now we're going to jump forward to chapter 20, where the Israelites are grumbling again...

It would have been better if we'd died!

Why did you bring us into this miserable place?

There's not even any water to drink!

READ
Numbers 20v1-11

Answers: 1—ten plagues, 2—God gives manna, 3—grumbling, 4—didn't trust God

---

What a terrible lot of moanalots!

Did they deserve God's kindness? **Yes / No**

But yet again, God is **merciful** to them.

Draw what happened when Moses struck the rock. (v11)

But that's not the end of the story!
More tomorrow...

PRAY

God was kind to the Israelites even though they didn't deserve it. __We__ don't deserve His kindness either. So spend some time thanking Him for it!

DAY 58 SAD SAGA

Spot the Difference. *There are eight to find.*

There <u>should</u> have been one more difference! Back in the book of Exodus, at a place called Rephidim, God <u>did</u> tell Moses to **strike** the rock. (*This story is in Exodus 17v1-7.*) But this time, God told Moses only to **speak** to the rock...

READ
Numbers 20v9-13

Moses was a good leader, who trusted God. But he wasn't **perfect**! This time Moses <u>didn't</u> obey God's command.

Only one man has ever lived a perfect life. Do you know who?

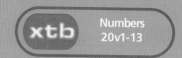 Numbers 20v1-13

Yesterday we saw that God was **merciful** to the Israelites. But what's the other side of the coin?

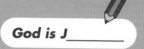

God is J_____

Mercy *God is merciful.* Justice *God is just.*

Because God is **just**, He punished Moses for his sin.

*Cross out the **X**'s to see how God punished him.*

XHXEXXWOXUXXLDXNXOXTXXENXTXERX

XTXHEXXPXROXXMXISXXEXDXXLXAXXNXDX

When the time came for the Israelites to enter the promised land of Canaan, Moses would <u>not</u> go with them.

PRAY Say sorry to God for times when <u>you</u> have disobeyed Him. Ask Him to help you to always trust Him and obey Him.

Answer: Only **Jesus** has ever lived a perfect life.

DAY 59 SAVED BY A SNAKE?

 Numbers 21v4-9

The Israelites are grumbling again...

READ
Numbers 21v4-9

The Israelites became impatient and started to **complain**. "Why did you bring us here to die? We hate this food!", they **grumbled**. Then God sent poisonous **snakes** among them. Many were bitten and died. So the people asked Moses to **pray** for them. God told Moses to make a snake on a pole. Anyone who was **bitten** could look at the bronze snake and be **healed**.

Fit all of the underlined words into the puzzle below to discover a hidden word.

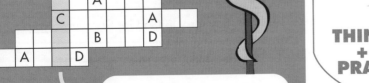

They sinned	The Israelites **complained** against God and accused Him of bringing them to the desert to die.
They were punished	So God sent deadly snakes to **punish** them.
God provided a way to be rescued	Those who looked at the bronze snake were **healed**.

Anyone who is bitten can look at the bronze snake and live. *Numbers 21v8*

THINK + PRAY

Mercy *God is merciful.* Justice *God is just.*

Because God is **just**, He sent the snakes to punish the Israelites. Because God is **merciful**, He gave them a way to be saved. Thank God that He is always both just and merciful.

DAY 60 SAVED BY JESUS

Jesus used the story of the snake on the pole to teach us about Himself...

READ
John 3v14-16

Fill in the gaps in Jesus' words.

life   Moses
believes
        snake

"Son of Man" is a title Jesus often used for Himself.

Just as **M**_____ lifted up the **s**_____ in the desert, so the Son of Man must be lifted up, so that everyone who **b**_____ in Him may have eternal **l**_____. (v14-15)

Crack the code to see what Jesus was saying about Himself.

C = ■   E = ■   J = ■   R = ●   T = ●
D = ■   I = ■   O = ●   S = ●   U = ●

___ ___ ___ ___ ___ ___   ___ ___ ___ ___

Jesus was "lifted up" to die on the cross, to rescue everyone who believes in Him.

We all sin — All of us sin. We do what <u>we</u> want instead of what <u>God</u> wants.

We deserve to be punished — The punishment for sin is death, and separation from God.

God provided a way to be rescued — Jesus came to die for us, to rescue us from our sin.

*To find out more turn to **The Servant King** opposite Day 12.*

Everyone who believes in me will have eternal life.
John 3v15

PRAY — **Father God, thank You for sending Jesus to die in my place so that I can be forgiven.**

DAY 61 JOURNEY'S END

STARTING OUT

At the beginning of Numbers, Moses took a census to count the people. *Flick back to chapter 1 to fill in the gaps.*

Numbers 1v1 → **Desert of S_____**

Numbers 1v46 → **Total number of men:**
_____

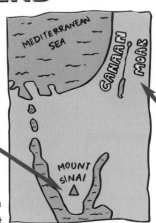

The Israelites had reached the edge of Canaan in just two months. But they were scared by what the 10 spies told them, and didn't <u>trust</u> God to give them the land. (Day 54)

Because they didn't trust God, they spent **40 years** wandering in the desert. During that time, God said that everyone who hadn't trusted Him would die.

*Draw their winding path through the desert, starting at **Mount Sinai** and ending in **Moab**.*

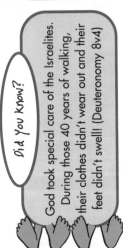

Did you know?

God took special care of the Israelites. During those 40 years of walking, their clothes didn't wear out and their feet didn't swell! (Deuteronomy 8v4)

FINISHING UP

At the end of Numbers, Moses took another census. *Flick forward to chapter 26 to fill in these gaps.*

Plains of M_____ ← Numbers 26v63

Total number of men: ← Numbers 26v51
_____

The two census totals are similar. But the actual people they counted were very different...

READ
Numbers 26v63-65

All the adults who <u>hadn't</u> trusted God had died, except for Moses, and two others. Who? (v65)

J_____ and **C_____**

They were saved because they <u>had</u> trusted God.

PRAY Everything happened just as God had said it would. Thank God that His words <u>always</u> come true.

DAY 62 NEW LEADER, SAME GOD

Moses' Maths
90+30 =
40×3 =
200-80 =
240÷2 =

Moses is now **120** years old! He knows that he won't lead the Israelites into the promised land of Canaan. Instead, they will have a <u>new</u> leader.

The Israelites will have a **new leader**. But it will be the **same God** who goes with them! There's no need to be afraid. ***God will never let them down!***

Copy verse 6 here.

Take the first letter of each picture to discover his name.

— — — — — —

READ
Deuteronomy 31v1-8

Did you know?

Joshua was one of the **12 spies** who explored Canaan 40 years earlier. He and Caleb were the only two who <u>trusted</u> God.

PRAY

If you are a Christian, then this promise is for you too. How does that make you feel? Talk to God about it.

DAY 63 A PEOPLE SAVED BY GOD

Moses is near the end of his life. Before he dies, he tells the Israelites **God's Law** again (the ten commandments and other laws).

They'll need to know how to live for God when they enter Canaan. *We can read Moses' words in Deuteronomy.*

Did you know?

Deuteronomy means "second law". In this book, Moses tells the Israelites God's Law for the <u>second</u> time.

Read the very last of Moses' words…

READ
Deuteronomy 33v29

Fill in the gaps.

saved   no one   LORD

There is _____ like you, a people _____ by the _____.

The Israelites weren't like anyone else. They were **unique**! Not because they were especially <u>good</u> (we know they weren't!), but because they'd been **chosen** by God.

• He'd **saved** them from Egypt.
• And was bringing them to Canaan.
• Just as He'd **promised**.

People Code

🧑=A   🧑=C   🧑=H   🧑=I

😠=N   🧑=R   🧑=S   🧧=T

But someone else can also be called "a people saved by the LORD". *Crack the people code to find out who.*

If you're a Christian, then <u>you</u> have been saved by God too. **Not** because you've been especially good. But because **Jesus** died for you as your Rescuer.

THINK+PRAY

Moses reminded the Israelites of all that God had done for them. They should **praise** and **thank** Him— and **obey** His law. The same is true for <u>you and me</u>. If you are a Christian, **praise** and **thank** God for saving you. Ask Him to help you to **obey** Him, and live His way.

LOOKING ON

When Moses had finished teaching the Israelites, he climbed to the top of a nearby mountain. From there, God showed him the whole of the promised land of Canaan.

READ
Deuteronomy 34v4-9

Moses saw the promised land, and knew that God would bring the Israelites safely there. But Moses didn't go with them. He died on the mountain.

How old was Moses when he died? (v7)

Who buried him? (v6)

Who became the new leader of the Israelites? (v9)

THINK SPOT

Think back over the life of Moses. Do you want to be like him? In what ways?

The books of Numbers and Deuteronomy teach us about God's character. Choose some words that describe what **God is like**. *Add more of your own.*

loving   merciful   just

          powerful   uncaring

faithless   faithful

          weak

PRAY

Thank God for the things you've learned about Him. Ask Him to help you to know Him better and better as you read His Word, the Bible.

THE PROMISE KEEPER

DAY 65

There had never been anyone like Moses...

READ
Deuteronomy 34v10-12

 There had never been a **prophet** (God's messenger) like **Moses**. God rescued him from Pharaoh when he was a baby. Much later, God spoke to him from the **burning bush** and sent him back to **Egypt** to perform miracles and **rescue** the Israelites. Moses was given the ten commandments on Mount Sinai, and taught the people God's **Law**. He led them through the **desert** for 40 years, and then taught them the Law again before he died.

Find all the underlined words in the wordsearch.

B	P	R	O	P	H	E	T
U	J	E	U	C	S	E	R
S	B	U	R	N	I	N	G
H	E	T	R	E	S	E	D
E	G	Y	P	T	S	U	S
L	A	W	S	E	S	O	M

Moses was a prophet (God's messenger) and a great leader. But earlier in Deuteronomy God had promised to send <u>another</u> prophet. (Deuteronomy 18v15+18)

This prophet would be far greater than Moses. *Use the leftover letters in the wordsearch to discover his name.*

_ _ _ _ _ _

In the Old Testament, God made many great promises...
- He would send a new **King**
- He would send a **Rescuer**
- He would send someone who would be God's way of **blessing** the whole world
- And He would send a **prophet** like Moses.

Wow! All of these promises came true when God sent *Jesus!*

PRAY

God promised that Jesus would come—and He did! He came as **Prophet**, **King** and **Rescuer**, to **bless** the whole world—just as God had said. Thank God, the Promise Keeper, for sending Jesus.

TIME FOR MORE?

Have you read all 65 days of XTB? Well done if you have!

How often do you use XTB?
- Every day?
- Nearly every day?
- Two or three times a week?
- Now and then?

You can use XTB at any time...

In the morning.

At bedtime.

When you get back from school.

When do YOU read XTB?

XTB comes out every three months. If you've been using it every day, or nearly every day, that's great! You may still have a few weeks to wait before you get the next issue of XTB. But don't worry!—that's what the extra readings are for...

EXTRA READINGS
The next four pages contain some extra Bible readings about prayer. If you read one each day, they will take you 26 days. Or you may want to read two or three each day. Or just pick a few to try. Whichever suits you best. There's a cracking wordsearch to solve too...

Drop us a line...
Why not write in and tell us what you think of XTB:
—What do you like best?
—Was there something you didn't understand?
—And any ideas for how we can make it better!

Write to: XTB, The Good Book Company, Blenheim House, 1 Blenheim Road, Epsom, Surrey, KT19 9AP
or e-mail me: alison@thegoodbook.co.uk

The extra readings start on the next page

TIME TO PRAY...

Do you find praying difficult? Do you wonder what to say? Or what to pray about? In these extra readings we're going to see what the Bible says about prayer.

Why do we say Amen?

We don't have to use special words when we pray. But people often do finish with **Amen**. It means "truly" or "I agree". That's why we say it at the end of someone else's prayer. It's like saying, "I agree, that's what I want to pray too."

The ideas in the box will help you as you read the verses.

PRAY Ask God to help you to understand what you read.

READ Read the Bible verses, and fill in the missing word in the puzzle.

THINK Think about what you have just read. Try to work out one main thing the writer is saying.

PRAY Thank God for what you have learned about Him.

There are 26 Bible readings on the next three pages. Part of each reading has been printed for you—but with a word missing. Fill in the missing words as you read the verses. Then see if you can find them all in the wordsearch below. Some are written backwards—or diagonally!

If you get stuck, check the answers at the end of Reading 26.

E	B	F	S	H	E	P	H	E	R	D	T	E	T	F
A	A	O	K	W	O	R	R	Y	B	E	H	V	R	A
R	G	R	E	A	T	A	O	T	A	E	A	O	O	I
N	O	G	L	O	R	Y	X	C	K	D	N	L	U	T
E	O	I	B	Y	E	E	H	A	N	S	K	M	B	H
S	D	V	N	I	A	R	A	T	O	S	F	A	L	F
T	K	E	X	T	B	G	O	D	W	I	U	R	E	U
L	N	D	A	Y	S	G	N	I	K	N	L	Y	Y	L
Y	O	U	R	P	E	O	P	L	E	G	R	G	P	N
T	W	O	C	C	A	S	I	O	N	I	A	N	P	E
A	L	T	R	U	M	P	E	T	S	N	I	I	A	S
G	E	T	H	S	E	M	A	N	E	G	N	K	H	S

Verses about when to pray and what about

Tick the box when you have read the verses.

1 ☐ **Read Mark 1v35**

If you have a busy day—how about getting up early to pray? Jesus did! "Very e _ _ _ _ in the morning, long before daylight, Jesus got up and left the house. He went out to a lonely place, where He prayed." (v35)

2 ☐ **Read Philippians 4v6-7**

We can pray about everything. We don't need to worry. "Don't w _ _ _ _ about anything, but in all your prayers ask God for what you need, always asking Him with a thankful heart."(v6)

3 ☐ **Read Ephesians 6v18**

We can pray at all times, wherever we are or whatever we are doing. "Pray on every o _ _ _ _ _ _ as the Spirit leads." (v18)

4 ☐ **Read Colossians 4v2**

Keep on praying. Don't give up! "Be persistent in p _ _ _ _ _ and keep alert as you pray, giving thanks to God." (v2)

5 ☐ **Read 1 Thessalonians 5v16-18**

We can pray to God anywhere, any time. There's loads to thank Him for, even when things seem hard. "Be joyful always, pray at all times, be t _ _ _ _ _ _ _ in all circumstances." (v16-18)

6 ☐ **Read Psalm 139v1-6**

God knows all about us before we pray, and He knows what we'll say. "LORD, you have examined me and you K _ _ _ me." (v1)

7 ☐ **Read James 5v13**

If you're in trouble, pray about it. If you're happy, also pray about it! —thanking and praising God. "Is anyone among you in t _ _ _ _ _ _ ? He should pray. Is anyone h _ _ _ _ ? He should sing praises." (v13)

8 ☐ **Read Colossians 4v2-4**

Pray for people who tell others about Jesus. Ask God to give them opportunities to speak for Him. "Pray also for us, that G _ _ may open a door for our message." (v3)

9 ☐ **Read 1 Timothy 2v1-2**

We should pray for those who lead our country. "I urge that petitions, prayers, requests and thanksgivings be offered to God for all people; for k _ _ _ _ and all others who are in authority." (v1-2))

10 ☐ **Read John 15v12**

Don't worry when you don't know how or what to pray. God's Holy Spirit will help you.

"We do not k _ _ _ what we ought to pray for, but the Spirit Himself pleads with God " (v12)

11 ☐ **Read Luke 11v1-4**

Jesus taught His followers how to pray. (Often called The Lord's Prayer.)

"Lord, t _ _ _ _ us to pray, just as John taught his disciples." (v1)

12 ☐ **Read Psalm 117v1-2**

Sometimes prayers are very short. Read the whole of Psalm 117 (the shortest psalm) aloud.

"His love for us is strong and His f _ _ _ _ _ _ _ _ _ _ _ is eternal." (v34)

Verses giving examples of prayer

13 ☐ **Read Mark 14v32-36**

Just before He was arrested, Jesus took time to pray.

"They came to a place called G _ _ _ _ _ _ _ _ _ and Jesus said to His disciples, "Sit here while I pray."" (v32)

14 ☐ **Read Luke 23v33-34**

While Jesus was being crucified, He prayed for the people who did it.

"Jesus said, 'F _ _ _ _ _ _ them, Father. They don't know what they are doing.'" (v34)

15 ☐ **Read Acts 1v14**

After the resurrection, when Jesus went up to heaven, His followers met frequently to pray together.

"They all joined together constantly in prayer, along with the women and M _ _ _ the mother of Jesus and with His brothers." (v14)

16 ☐ **Read Acts 12v5**

When Peter was arrested by Herod, the other Christians prayed for him. You can read about the answer to their prayers in Acts 12v6-19.

"So Peter was kept in jail, but the people of the church were praying e _ _ _ _ _ _ _ _ to God for him." (v5)

17 ☐ **Read Acts 16v25**

Paul and Silas were thrown in prison for teaching about Jesus. But even so, they were praying and singing!

"About midnight Paul and Silas were praying and s _ _ _ _ _ _ hymns to God." (v25)

18 ☐ **Read James 5v17-18**

Elijah was just like us. But look how God answered his prayer!

"Elijah was the same kind if person as we are. He prayed earnestly that there would be no r _ _ _ and no r _ _ _ fell on the land for three and a half years." (v17)

Reading Psalms aloud as prayers

19 ☐ **Read Psalm 23v1-6**

You may know a tune for this psalm. If so sing it, if not read it aloud.
"The LORD is my
s _ _ _ _ _ _ _ ." (v1)

20 ☐ **Read Psalm 19v1-6**

Look at the sky—then praise God (He designed the sky!) for being so great.
"How clearly the sky reveals God's
g _ _ _ _ !" (v1)

21 ☐ **Read Psalm 150v1-6**

If you can play an instrument, play a tune to praise God. Otherwise clap your hands as you read this psalm.
Praise Him with
_ _ _ _ _ _ _ . Praise Him with harps and lyres." (v3)

22 ☐ **Read Psalm 136v1**

Every line of this psalm ends with the same words, thanking God for His everlasting love.
"Give thanks to the LORD, for He is good; His l _ _ _ is eternal." (v1)

23 ☐ **Read Psalm 47v1-9**

When we pray, we are talking to the King of the whole world!
"God is K _ _ _ over all the world." (v7)

24 ☐ **Read Psalm 100v1-5**

If we are Christians, then we are God's people. He looks after us like a shepherd takes care of his sheep.
"We are His p _ _ _ _ _ _ , we are His flock." (v3)

25 ☐ **Read Psalm 96v1-3**

If you're a Christian, ask God to help you to tell your friends about Him. This psalm says we should tell the whole world about God saving us.
"Proclaim His glory to the nations, His mighty d _ _ _ _ to all peoples." (v3)

26 ☐ **Read Psalm 96v4-6**

We should praise and thank God because He is the Greatest!
"The Lord is g _ _ _ _ and is to be highly praised." (v4)

WHAT NEXT?

XTB comes out every three months. Each issue contains 65 full XTB pages, plus 26 days of extra readings. By the time you've used them all, the next issue of XTB will be available.

ISSUE SIX OF XTB

Issue Six of XTB explores the books of Mark, Joshua and Ephesians.

- Investigate <u>who</u> Jesus is and <u>why</u> He came in **Mark's** Gospel.
- The Israelites reach the promised land at last in the Book of **Joshua**—but battles await them!
- Read the end of Paul's prison letter to the **Ephesians**.

Available from your local Good Book Company website:

UK: www.thegoodbook.co.uk
North America: www.thegoodbook.com
Australia: www.thegoodbook.com.au
New Zealand: www.thegoodbook.co.nz

XTB Prayer Diary

Don't worry if you've lost your XTB Prayer Diary. We've printed some of the pages below, and inside the back cover.

HOW TO PRAY

Prayer is talking to God.
- You don't have to use special words.
- You can pray out loud.
- Or you can pray quietly in your head.

Some people **kneel down**—to remind them how <u>great</u> God is—and **close their eyes**—to help them <u>think carefully</u> about what they're praying. But you don't have to!

Find a time and place where you can be quiet for a few minutes. Your room is often a good choice. But you can pray anywhere—in the garden, as you walk to school, or even up a tree!

> Wherever you choose, God is always there. And He's always ready to listen.

Do you have any questions?
...about anything you've read in XTB.
—send them in and we'll do our best to answer them.

Do you know any good jokes?
—send them in and they might appear in XTB!

Write to: XTB, The Good Book Company, Blenheim House, 1 Blenheim R
Epsom, Surrey, KT19 9AP, UK **or e-mail me:** alison@thegoodbook.co.